the 20th Century
Movie Music

ISBN 0-634-02194-X

HAL•LEONARD®
CORPORATION

7777 W. BLUEMOUND RD. P.O. BOX 13819 MILWAUKEE, WI 53213

Visit Hal Leonard Online at
www.halleonard.com

CONTENTS

AROUND THE WORLD
from AROUND THE WORLD IN EIGHTY DAYS

Words and Music by VICTOR YOUNG
and HAROLD ADAMSON

BUTTONS AND BOWS

from the Paramount Picture PALEFACE

Words and Music by JAY LIVINGSTON
and RAY EVANS

8

BE A CLOWN
from THE PIRATE

Words and Music by
COLE PORTER

Brightly

I'll re-mem-ber for-ev-er, when I was but three, Ma-ma, who was clev-er re-mark-ing to me: "If, son, when you're grown up, you

THEME FROM "CASINO ROYALE"

from CASINO ROYALE

Words by HAL DAVID
Music by BURT BACHARACH

got us on the run   with guns ___   and knives. ___

We're fight-ing for our lives.

Have no fear, Bond is here.

Repeat and Fade

He's gon-na save the world. Bond is here, have no fear!

CHARIOTS OF FIRE
from CHARIOTS OF FIRE

Music by VANGELIS

CHANGE THE WORLD
featured on the Motion Picture Soundtrack PHENOMENON

Words and Music by WAYNE KIRKPATRICK,
GORDON KENNEDY and TOMMY SIMS

CHEEK TO CHEEK
from the RKO Radio Motion Picture TOP HAT

Words and Music by
IRVING BERLIN

COUNT YOUR BLESSINGS INSTEAD OF SHEEP

from the Motion Picture Irving Berlin's WHITE CHRISTMAS

Words and Music by
IRVING BERLIN

When I'm wor-ried and I can't sleep, __ I count my bless-ings in-stead of sheep. __ And I fall a sleep __ count-ing my bless-ings. __ When my bank-roll is

COLE'S SONG

from MR. HOLLAND'S OPUS

Words by JULIAN LENNON and JUSTIN CLAYTON
Music by MICHAEL KAMEN

DO YOU KNOW WHERE YOU'RE GOING TO?

Theme from MAHOGANY

Words by GERRY GOFFIN
Music by MIKE MASSER

42

Now _____ look-ing back at all _____ we planned,

we let _____ so man - y dreams _ just slip through our _____ hands. _

44

ENDLESS LOVE
from ENDLESS LOVE

Words and Music by
LIONEL RICHIE

they tell me how much you __ care. ____ Oh,
you mean the world to __ me. ____ Oh,

__ yes, you will al - ways be
I know you will al I've found __ in you

my end - less love. ____
my end - less

love. ____

49

Oh, _____ and _ love, _____

FOOTLOOSE
Theme from the Paramount Motion Picture FOOTLOOSE

Words by DEAN PITCHFORD and KENNY LOGGINS
Music by KENNY LOGGINS

58

GEORGY GIRL
from GEORGY GIRL

Words by JIM DALE
Music by TOM SPRINGFIELD

FORREST GUMP – MAIN TITLE
(Feather Theme)
from the Paramount Motion Picture FORREST GUMP

Music by ALAN SILVESTRI

8va

f

(lightly)

THE GODFATHER
(Love Theme)
from the Paramount Picture THE GODFATHER

By NINO ROTA

Slowly and expressively

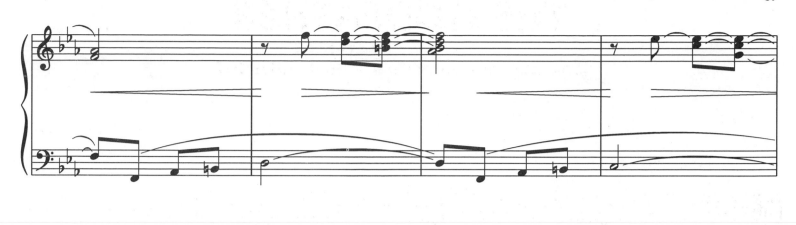

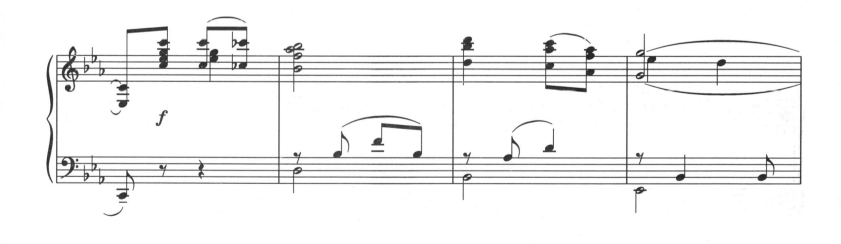

HAKUNA MATATA
from Walt Disney Pictures' THE LION KING

Music by ELTON JOHN
Lyrics by TIM RICE

A HARD DAY'S NIGHT

from A HARD DAY'S NIGHT

Words and Music by JOHN LENNON
and PAUL McCARTNEY

C

D

get home to you____ I find the thing that you do____ will make me
love to come home____ 'Cause when I get you a - lone____ you know I'll

G **C9** **1 G** To Coda ⊕ **2 G** **Bm**

feel____ al - right.____ You know I
be____ O. K.____ When I'm home____

Em **Bm** **G**

ev - 'ry - thing seems to be al - right. When I'm home____

Em **C** **D**

feel - ing you hold - ing me tight, tight, yeah, It's been a

Em   Bm   G

ev-'ry-thing seems to be al-right.   When I'm home

Em   C   D
                                        D.S. al Coda

feel-ing you hold-ing me tight,   tight,   yeah,   It's been a

CODA   G   C9   G

You know I feel al - right,   You know I

C(add9)   F(add9)
                                        Repeat and Fade

feel al-right.

HOW DEEP IS YOUR LOVE

from the Motion Picture SATURDAY NIGHT FEVER

Words and Music by BARRY GIBB,
MAURICE GIBB and ROBIN GIBB

HYMN TO THE FALLEN
from the Paramount and DreamWorks Motion Picture SAVING PRIVATE RYAN

Music by JOHN WILLIAMS

Slowly, reverently

Broadly and expansively

I BELIEVE IN YOU AND ME

from the Touchstone Motion Picture THE PREACHER'S WIFE

Words and Music by DAVID WOLFERT
and SANDY LINZER

I SAY A LITTLE PRAYER

featured in the TriStar Motion Picture MY BEST FRIEND'S WEDDING

Lyric by HAL DAVID
Music by BURT BACHARACH

(1.) The mo - ment I wake up,
(2.) I run ___ for the bus, dear.
(D.S.) *Instrumental solo*

be - fore ___ I put on my make - up,
While rid - ing, I think of us, dear.

I
I
(I

I WILL REMEMBER YOU

Theme from THE BROTHERS McMULLEN

Words and Music by SARAH McLACHLAN,
SEAMUS EGAN and DAVE MERENDA

IF I HAD A TALKING PICTURE OF YOU

from SUNNY SIDE UP

Words and Music by RAY HENDERSON,
LEW BROWN and B.G. DeSYLVA

110

IL POSTINO
(The Postman)
from IL POSTINO

Music by LUIS BACALOV

Moderato

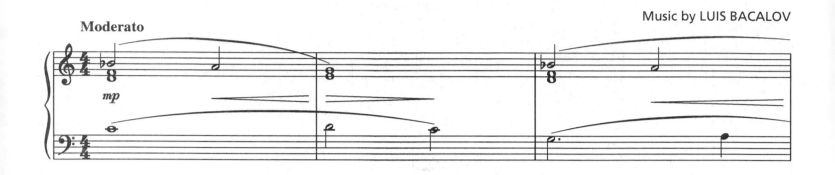

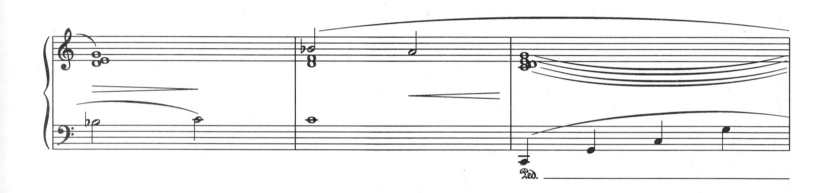

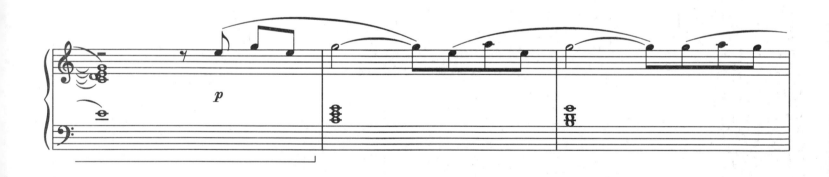

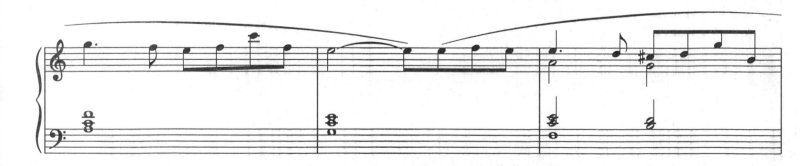

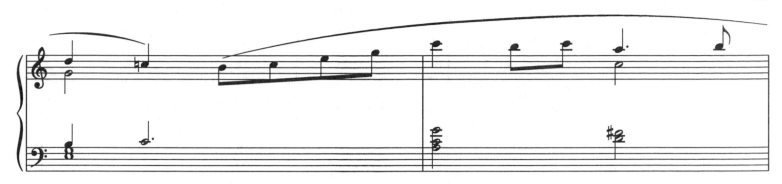

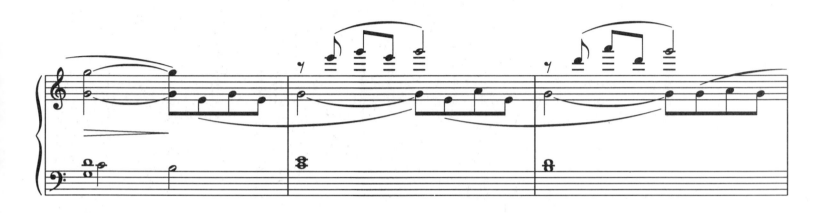

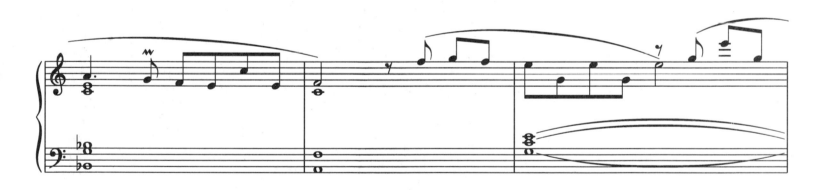

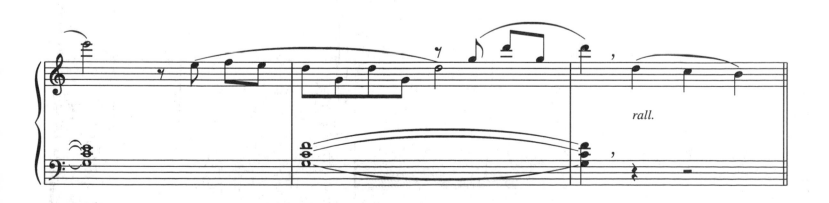

A Tempo

IRIS
from the Motion Picture CITY OF ANGELS

Words and Music by
JOHN RZEZNIK

And I _____ don't want the world _____ to see _____ me

ISN'T IT ROMANTIC?

from the Paramount Picture LOVE ME TONIGHT

Words by LORENZ HART
Music by RICHARD RODGERS

JESSICA'S THEME
(Breaking In the Colt)
from THE MAN FROM SNOWY RIVER

By BRUCE ROWLAND

To Coda $\oplus$

D.S. al Coda

CODA

THE JOHN DUNBAR THEME
from DANCES WITH WOLVES

By JOHN BARRY

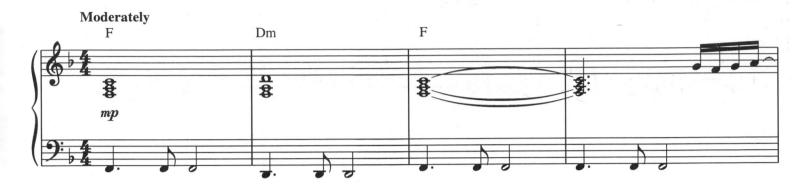

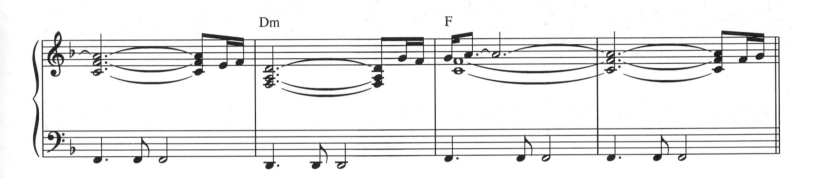

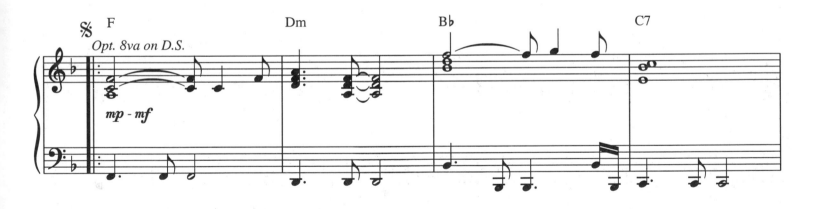

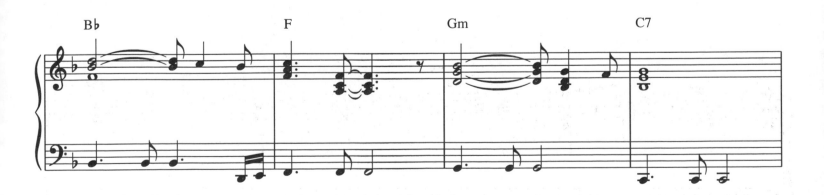

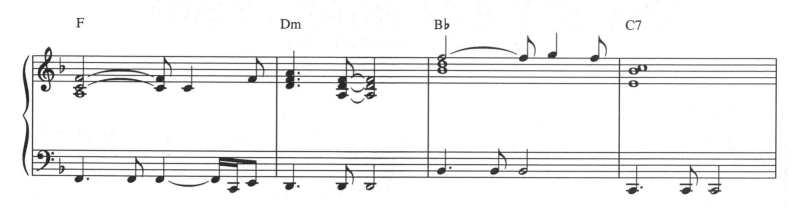

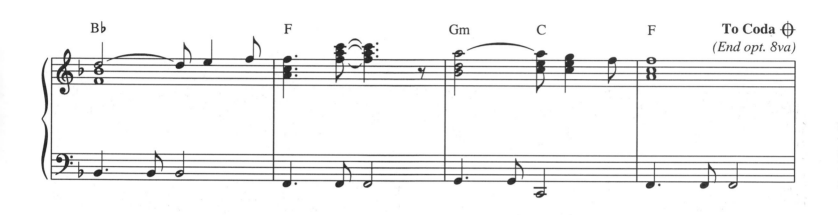

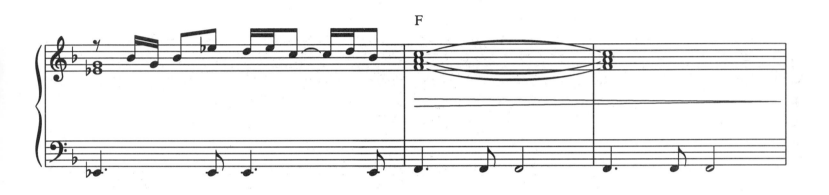

LAST DANCE
from THANK GOD IT'S FRIDAY

Words and Music by
PAUL JABARA

LES POISSONS
from Walt Disney's THE LITTLE MERMAID

Lyrics by HOWARD ASHMAN
Music by ALAN MENKEN

love lit - tle fish - es, don't you?_____ Here's

some - thing for tempt - ing the pal - ate, _____ Pre - pared in the

clas - sic tech - nique. First you pound the fish flat with a

mal - let. _____ Then you slash through the skin, give the bel - ly a

LET'S GO FLY A KITE

from Walt Disney's MARY POPPINS

Words and Music by RICHARD M. SHERMAN
and ROBERT B. SHERMAN

LOVE ME TENDER

from LOVE ME TENDER

Words and Music by ELVIS PRESLEY
and VERA MATSON

Love me ten - der, love me sweet,
Love me ten - der, love me long,
Love me ten - der, love me dear,
When at last my dreams come true,

nev - er let me go. You have made my
take me to your heart, for it's there that
tell me you are mine. I'll be yours through
dar - ling, this I know: Hap - pi - ness will

LOVE STORY
Theme from the Paramount Picture LOVE STORY

Music by FRANCIS LAI

THE MAN FROM SNOWY RIVER
(Main Title Theme)
from THE MAN FROM SNOWY RIVER

By BRUCE ROWLAND

THE MAN THAT GOT AWAY
from the Motion Picture A STAR IS BORN

Lyric by IRA GERSHWIN
Music by HAROLD ARLEN

CODA

MISSION: IMPOSSIBLE THEME

from the Paramount Motion Picture MISSION: IMPOSSIBLE

By LALO SCHIFRIN

Moderate Dance beat, with drive

To Coda ⊕

MOON RIVER
from the Paramount Picture BREAKFAST AT TIFFANY'S

Words by JOHNNY MERCER
Music by HENRY MANCINI

MORE
(Ti guardero' nel cuore)
from the film MONDO CANE

Music by NINO OLIVIERO and RIZ ORTOLANI
Italian Lyrics by MARCELLO CIORCIOLINI
English Lyrics by NORMAN NEWELL

MY HEART WILL GO ON

(Love Theme from 'Titanic')

from the Paramount and Twentieth Century Fox Motion Picture TITANIC

Music by JAMES HORNER
Lyric by WILL JENNINGS

Lyrics:
Ev-'ry night in my dreams _____ I see you, I feel you, that is how I

PART OF YOUR WORLD

from Walt Disney's THE LITTLE MERMAID

Lyrics by HOWARD ASHMAN
Music by ALAN MENKEN

RAIDERS MARCH
from the Paramount Motion Picture RAIDERS OF THE LOST ARK

Music by JOHN WILLIAMS

With animated precision

RAINDROPS KEEP FALLIN' ON MY HEAD

from BUTCH CASSIDY AND THE SUNDANCE KID

Lyric by HAL DAVID
Music by BURT BACHARACH

REFLECTION
(Pop Version)
from Walt Disney Pictures' MULAN
As Performed by Christina Aguilera

Music by MATTHEW WILDER
Lyrics by DAVID ZIPPEL

Look at me, you may think you see who I really am, but you'll nev-er know me. Ev-'ry day it's as if I play a part.

THE RIVER KWAI MARCH
from THE BRIDGE ON THE RIVER KWAI

By MALCOLM ARNOLD

ROMEO AND JULIET
(Love Theme)
from the Paramount Picture ROMEO AND JULIET

By NINO ROTA

ROCK AROUND THE CLOCK

featured in the Motion Picture AMERICAN GRAFFITI

Swing shuffle

Words and Music by MAX C. FREEDMAN
and JIMMY DeKNIGHT

One, two, three o'-clock, four o'-clock rock. Five six, sev-en o'-clock, eight o'-clock rock. Nine, ten, e-lev-en o'-clock, twelve o'-clock rock, we're gon-na rock a-round the clock to-night.__ 1. Put your

glad rags on and join me, Hon.__ We'll have some fun when the
clock strikes two and three and four,__ if the band slows down we'll__
chimes ring five and six and seven,__ we'll be rock-in' up in ___
eight, nine, ten, e-lev-en, too,__ I'll be go-in' strong and __
clock strikes twelve, we'll cool off, then,__ start a rock-in' 'round the ___

SHE
from NOTTING HILL

Lyric by HERBERT KRETZMER
Music by CHARLES AZNAVOUR

Moderately

SOMETHING GOOD
from THE SOUND OF MUSIC

Lyrics and Music by
RICHARD RODGERS

218

STAR TREK® THE MOTION PICTURE

Theme from the Paramount Picture STAR TREK: THE MOTION PICTURE

Music by JERRY GOLDSMITH

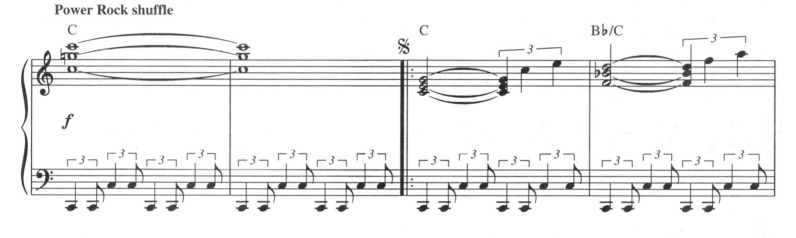

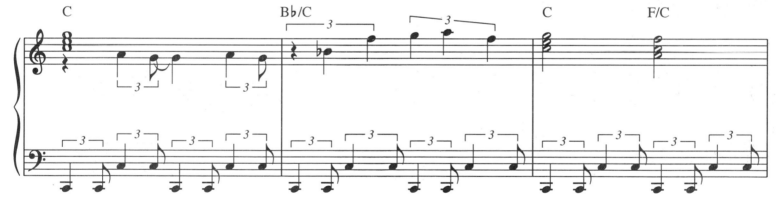

SOMEWHERE, MY LOVE
Lara's Theme from DOCTOR ZHIVAGO

Lyric by PAUL FRANCIS WEBSTER
Music by MAURICE JARRE

hill

blos - soms in green and gold,

and there are dreams all that your heart can

hold. Some - day _____ we'll meet a -

gain, my love. Some - day _____

STEPPIN' OUT WITH MY BABY
from the Motion Picture Irving Berlin's EASTER PARADE

Words and Music by
IRVING BERLIN

SUPERCALIFRAGILISTICEXPIALIDOCIOUS
from Walt Disney's MARY POPPINS

Words and Music by RICHARD M. SHERMAN
and ROBERT B. SHERMAN

MARY POPPINS
Sup - er - cal - i - frag - il - is - tic - ex - pi - al - i - do - cious!

E - ven though the sound of it is some - thing quite a - tro - cious,

If you say it loud e - nough, you'll al - ways sound pre - co - cious.

TEARS IN HEAVEN

featured in the Motion Picture RUSH

Words and Music by ERIC CLAPTON
and WILL JENNINGS

Be-yond the door ___ there's peace, I'm sure, _

THAT'S AMORÉ
(That's Love)
from the Paramount Picture THE CADDY
featured in the Motion Picture MOONSTRUCK

Words by JACK BROOKS
Music by HARRY WARREN

THANKS FOR THE MEMORY
from the Paramount Picture BIG BROADCAST OF 1938

Words and Music by LEO ROBIN
and RALPH RAINGER

THAT'S ENTERTAINMENT
from THE BAND WAGON

Words by HOWARD DIETZ
Music by ARTHUR SCHWARTZ

THREE COINS IN THE FOUNTAIN

from THREE COINS IN THE FOUNTAIN

Words by SAMMY CAHN
Music by JULE STYNE

TOP HAT, WHITE TIE AND TAILS

from the RKO Radio Motion Picture TOP HAT

Words and Music by
IRVING BERLIN

UNCHAINED MELODY
featured in the Motion Picture GHOST

Lyric by HY ZARET
Music by ALEX NORTH

Tempo I

THE WAY WE WERE

from the Motion Picture THE WAY WE WERE

Words by ALAN and MARILYN BERGMAN
Music by MARVIN HAMLISCH

WHEN SHE LOVED ME

from Walt Disney Pictures' TOY STORY 2 - A Pixar Film

Music and Lyrics by
RANDY NEWMAN

270

WHEN YOU BELIEVE

(from THE PRINCE OF EGYPT)

Words and Music Composed by STEPHEN SCHWARTZ
with Additional Music by BABYFACE

A WINK AND A SMILE

featured in the TriStar Motion Picture SLEEPLESS IN SEATTLE

Music by MARC SHAIMAN
Lyrics by RAMSEY McLEAN

1. I re-mem-ber the days of just keep-ing time, of
2. (Instrumental solo ad lib...

hang-ing a-round in sleep-y towns for-ev-er; ...end solo)

back roads emp-ty for miles.
Give me a wink and a smile.

Well, you
(continue solo...

A WHOLE NEW WORLD

from Walt Disney's ALADDIN

Music by ALAN MENKEN
Lyrics by TIM RICE

YELLOW SUBMARINE

from YELLOW SUBMARINE

Words and Music by JOHN LENNON
and PAUL McCARTNEY

Chorus:

YOU'LL BE IN MY HEART

(Pop Version)

from Walt Disney Pictures' TARZAN™
As Performed by Phil Collins

Words and Music by
PHIL COLLINS

YOUNG AT HEART

from YOUNG AT HEART

Words by CAROLYN LEIGH
Music by JOHNNY RICHARDS